MINECRAFT™

WORLDS
NEW YORK

Published in the United States by Random House Worlds, an imprint of Random House, a division of Penguin Random House LLC, New York.

RANDOM HOUSE is a registered trademark, and RANDOM HOUSE WORLDS and colophon are trademarks of Penguin Random House LLC.

Published in hardcover in the United Kingdom by Farshore, an imprint of HarperCollins Publishers Limited.

ISBN 978-0-593-97239-7
Ebook ISBN 978-0-593-97240-3

Printed in the United States on acid-free paper

randomhousebooks.com

2 4 6 8 9 7 5 3 1

First US Edition

Additional illustrations by George Lee
Special thanks to Sherin Kwan, Alex Wiltshire, Jay Castello, Kelsey Ranallo and Milo Bengtsson

MINECRAFT™

MEGA BITE-SIZE BUILDS

OVER 20 INCREDIBLE MINI PROJECTS

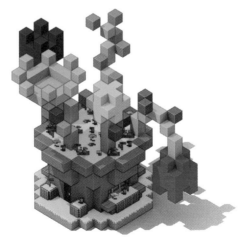

CONTENTS

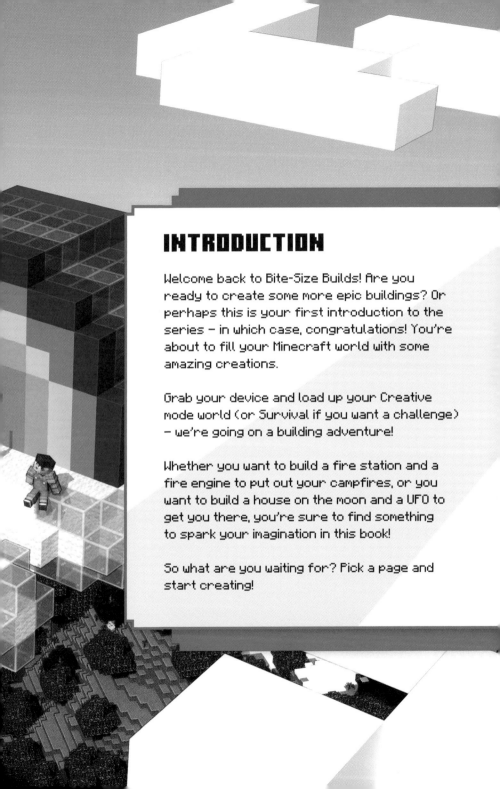

INTRODUCTION

Welcome back to Bite-Size Builds! Are you ready to create some more epic buildings? Or perhaps this is your first introduction to the series – in which case, congratulations! You're about to fill your Minecraft world with some amazing creations.

Grab your device and load up your Creative mode world (or Survival if you want a challenge) – we're going on a building adventure!

Whether you want to build a fire station and a fire engine to put out your campfires, or you want to build a house on the moon and a UFO to get you there, you're sure to find something to spark your imagination in this book!

So what are you waiting for? Pick a page and start creating!

GENERAL BUILD TIPS

Check out all the amazing builds in this book! There's really something for everyone, no matter your skill level. You can start with the easy builds or dive straight into one of the more complex builds. The choice is yours! Here are some tips to help you get started.

CREATIVE MODE

We recommend that you use Creative mode for these builds. With unlimited access to all the blocks in the game and instant block removal, Creative mode is the easiest way to build in Minecraft. If you like a challenge, each structure can be built in Survival mode, but be warned – it will take a lot more time and preparation!

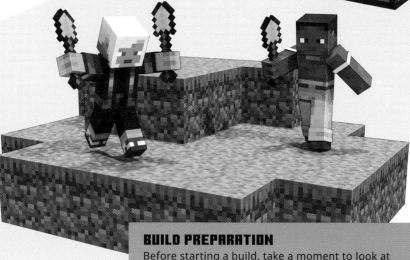

BUILD PREPARATION

Before starting a build, take a moment to look at the instructions. Consider where you want to place the structure and how much space you will need to complete it. You'll need to give yourself plenty of room to build!

TEMPORARY BLOCKS

Temporary building blocks are great for counting out spaces or placing floating items. Using temporary blocks will also help you with tricky block placement!

Count the dimensions using different color blocks. This row represents 11 blocks wide: 5 green + 6 yellow.

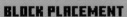

Use temporary blocks to help place floating blocks.

HOTBARS

Most builds use lots of different materials. You can prepare your blocks in the hotbar before starting for quick access, and if you don't have enough space, you can save up to nine hotbars in the inventory window.

BLOCK PLACEMENT

Placing a block beside an interactive one, such as an enchanting table, can be tricky. By clicking to place a block, you'll activate the interactive one instead. Thankfully, there is a trick to avoid this! Crouch first and then click to place your block. Simple!

FROG STATUE

Want a statue that will make every day a bit more ribbiting? Why not build this outside your base? Or better yet, add a door and you can even hop inside and make it your home. We've made this frog orange, but you could mix things up and build it in another color. It will be toadally awesome!

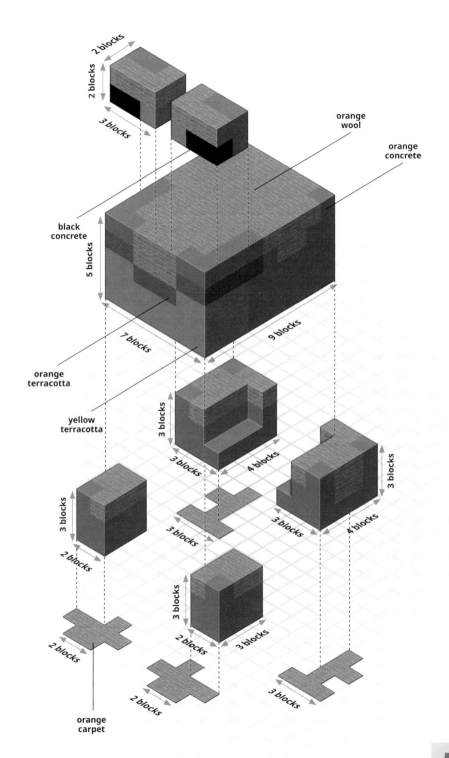

2 blocks

2 blocks

3 blocks

orange
wool

orange
concrete

black
concrete

5 blocks

orange
terracotta

7 blocks

9 blocks

yellow
terracotta

3 blocks

3 blocks

4 blocks

3 blocks

3 blocks

3 blocks

2 blocks

3 blocks

3 blocks

4 blocks

2 blocks

3 blocks

2 blocks

2 blocks

orange
carpet

2 blocks

3 blocks

9

HOUSE ON THE MOON

CALLING ALL CHEESE LOVERS! Did that get your attention? Good. Sorry, folks, this moon isn't actually made of cheese, but it is pretty brie-lliant! This is the ultimate base with a view. Build it high in the sky so you can watch over the Overworld from the comfort of your tiny moon cottage. Sweet!

DIFFICULTY:
★★★☆☆
🕐 30 mins

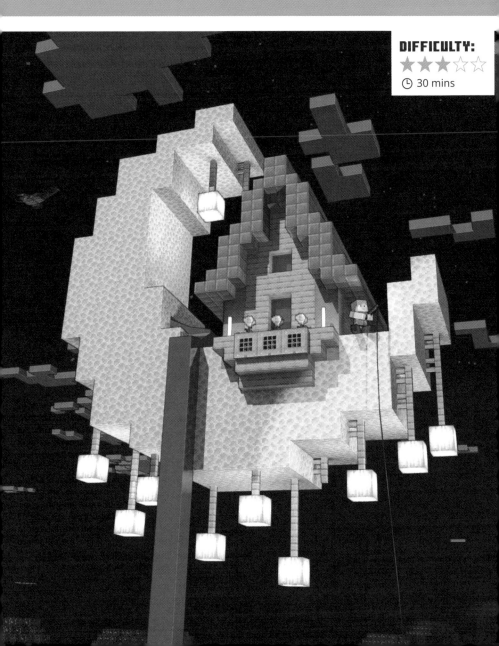

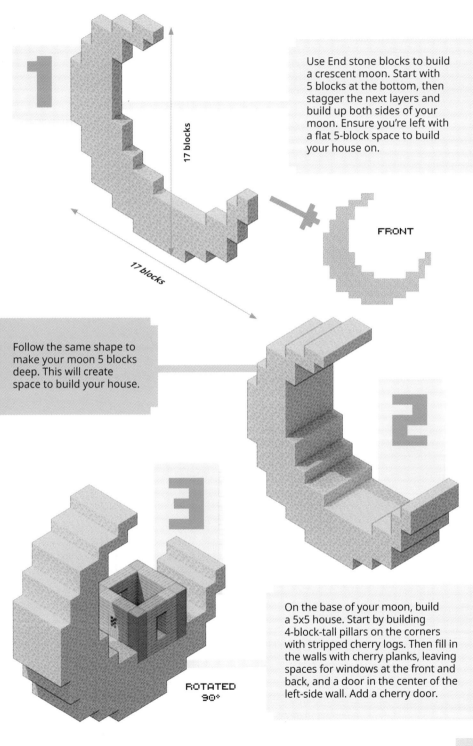

1

17 blocks

17 blocks

Use End stone blocks to build a crescent moon. Start with 5 blocks at the bottom, then stagger the next layers and build up both sides of your moon. Ensure you're left with a flat 5-block space to build your house on.

FRONT

Follow the same shape to make your moon 5 blocks deep. This will create space to build your house.

2

3

ROTATED 90°

On the base of your moon, build a 5x5 house. Start by building 4-block-tall pillars on the corners with stripped cherry logs. Then fill in the walls with cherry planks, leaving spaces for windows at the front and back, and a door in the center of the left-side wall. Add a cherry door.

4

Add an arch of cherry planks above your front and back walls, leaving a block gap above the windows. Add a stack of 2 cherry planks on the arch, then add purple stained glass panes to all the gaps.

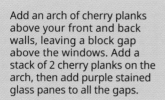

5

Time to build a cute planter on the front of your house. A block below the bottom window, place 3 upside-down cherry stairs. Above these, add 3 grass blocks and place 3 cherry trapdoors on the sides of them. Add 2 upside-down cherry stairs on either side, with End rods on top. Then plant 3 flowers.

Now let's build the roof. Use a mixture of purpur blocks and stairs, and follow the shape of the walls to build a staggered roof on top of your house. Finish it 1 block below the top of the walls.

6

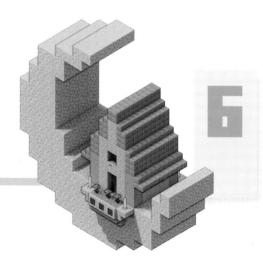

Extend the roof out 1 block to the front and back of your house, and add upside-down purpur stairs on the inside of the bottom of the roof.

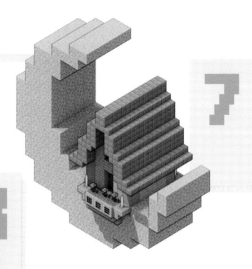

A moon house is not complete without stars! Use cherry fences to dangle verdant froglights from the moon, above and below your house.

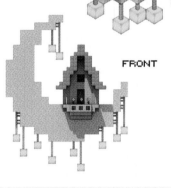

FRONT

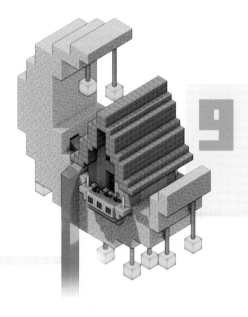

But how do you get up to your moon house? A ladder would be way too obvious. No, a waterfall is far cooler! Add a water source block to the left of the house by the door so that you can swim up to it.

SWORD PORTAL

What could be more epic than a ginormous sword piercing the ground with a Nether portal in it? Can't think of anything? Neither can we! This portal will be visible from many blocks away, so you'll always be able to find your way back to it when you fancy another Nether adventure.

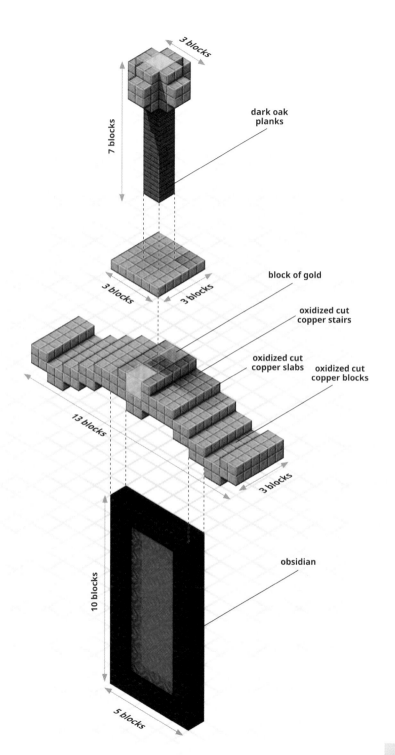

3 blocks

7 blocks

dark oak
planks

block of gold

3 blocks   3 blocks

oxidized cut
copper stairs

oxidized cut
copper slabs   oxidized cut
copper blocks

13 blocks

3 blocks

obsidian

10 blocks

5 blocks

15

FIRE STATION

Quick! Slide down the firefighter's pole and armor up – there's a fire to tackle! Oh, it's just another zombie on fire. When will they learn to seek shade when the sun rises? If you long for action, then this fire station is the build for you. You'll always be ready for an adventure!

DIFFICULTY:
★★★★☆
🕑 40 mins

1

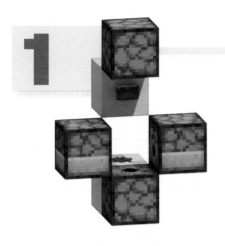

The fire station will need armor equippers so the firefighters are protected. Place 4 dispensers facing inward with a 1x2 space between them. In front of the bottom dispenser, place a white concrete block with redstone dust on top. Leave a space and then add another block above with a stone button on the side facing the dispensers.

Build another armor equipper beside your first and then add two more, 3 blocks opposite them. Fill the space between the bottom dispensers with gray concrete, then build up walls around your stations with white concrete, leaving spaces to enter them. Fill each dispenser with a different type of armor.

2

3

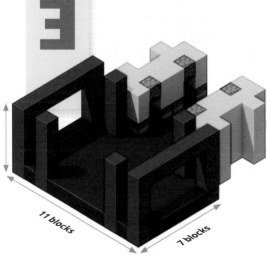

11 blocks

7 blocks

Beside your armor area, create another gray concrete floor that's 11x7 blocks. On the short sides of this rectangle, build two arches with red concrete, 4 blocks tall and 7 across. Then 2 blocks along from each vertical part of the arch, build a 4-block-tall pillar. Where each pillar and arch touches the floor level, replace the gray concrete with a red concrete block.

Using white concrete, fill in the space between the inner two pillars on the outer wall. Then, on the same level as the top of the arches and pillars, fill in the ceiling, leaving a 3x3 hole and another block space just inside the wall.

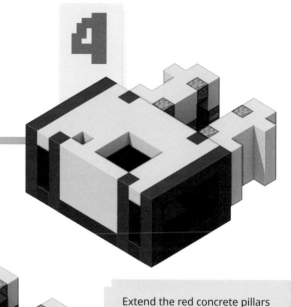

Extend the red concrete pillars up by 3 and fill the space in between them with white concrete on two sides and glass panes on the others. On the bottom floor, add glass panes to all of the gaps, leaving a 2x3 space for an entrance with iron bars on both sides.

Now you need to build somewhere to park your fire engine. Extend the floor of your armor area out 1 block with gray concrete, then add a 7x20 rectangle. Around the rectangle, add two layers of white concrete, leaving the front edge free. Add four pillars to the outside edges, 3 blocks in from each end.

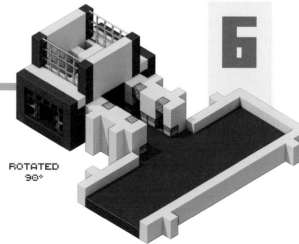

ROTATED 90°

Use brick blocks to extend the walls up by 6 blocks, and fill in the wall near the armor area. Replace random blocks with granite and polished granite for texture. Add a mixture of 4 brick and granite blocks to each pillar and top with brick or granite stairs. Inside the entrance, build an arch a block back with red concrete, the same height as the walls.

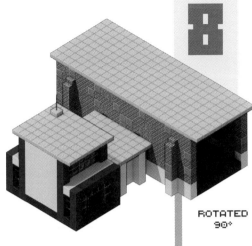

ROTATED 90°

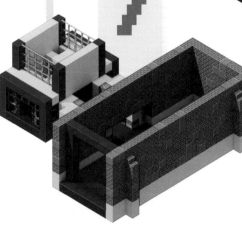

Use smooth stone slabs to add roofs to each of your sections, extending 1 block out at the front and back. On top of the main building, add a slab with an iron bar for an aerial.

INTERIORS

It wouldn't be an awesome fire station without a firefighter's pole to slide down! Just stack iron bars on top of each other between both levels of your station, and pop a slime block at the bottom to cushion the fall. Be sure to add a ladder so you can climb back up again! Finish off with a sofa upstairs made of cherry stairs, and decorate your armor equippers with item frames.

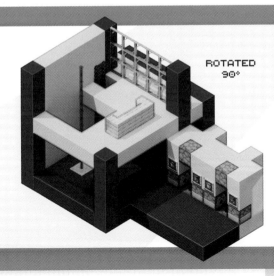

ROTATED 90°

19

FIRE ENGINE

Make way, make way! Fire engine coming through! Oh wait. It doesn't actually move. But don't let that stop you from building this incredible fire engine with a built-in swimming pool and diving board. It could be the most heroic swim of your life. Dive on in!

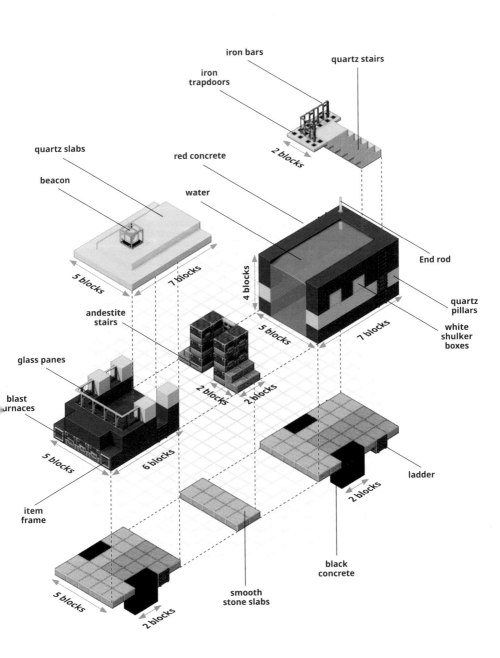

iron bars

iron trapdoors

quartz stairs

quartz slabs

red concrete

beacon

water

2 blocks

End rod

5 blocks

7 blocks

4 blocks

quartz pillars

andestite stairs

5 blocks

white shulker boxes

7 blocks

glass panes

2 blocks

2 blocks

blast furnaces

ladder

5 blocks

6 blocks

2 blocks

item frame

black concrete

5 blocks

smooth stone slabs

2 blocks

COLORFUL CASITA

Build a house for your friends and family with this gorgeous casita (little house)! Full of layers, colors and plants, this casita will be a jewel in the landscape, wherever you build it. All you have to decide is who's going to move in. There's sure to be a zombie that would accept!

DIFFICULTY:
★★★★☆

🕐 45 mins

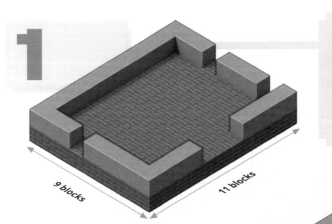

1 Start by building a 9x11 rectangle of acacia planks. On top of this, add the first layer of your walls with yellow terracotta, leaving spaces for 3 doors and a 3-block doorway.

9 blocks

11 blocks

Continue to build your walls up until they are 4 blocks tall. Make your door spaces 2 blocks tall and your doorway 3 blocks high. Then add two holes for windows to your back wall, 2 blocks tall.

2

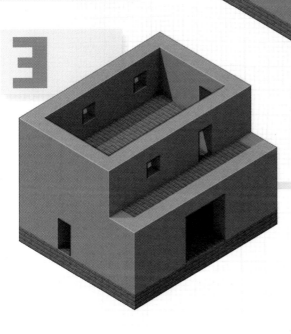

3

Fill in the ceiling with acacia planks, then add yellow terracotta walls on top, 2 blocks in from the front and 3 blocks tall. Add three holes for windows and two spaces for doors.

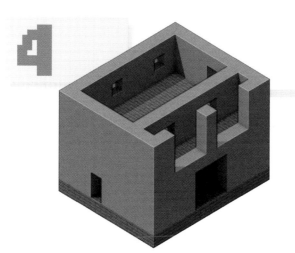

4

Extend your yellow terracotta walls out either side of your balcony, ending 1 block round the corners, then add a 3-block pillar in the center of the wall.

5

On top of the back-left corner of your casita, build a 5x5 square of cherry planks, 2 blocks tall.

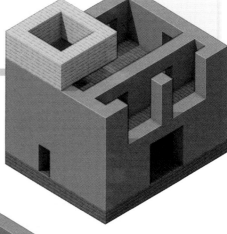

6

To the side of your build, add a ground-floor extension. First add a 4x7 rectangle of acacia planks in line with the back of the casita, then build walls 4 blocks high with lime terracotta, leaving holes for two windows.

Add an entrance hall to your casita. Place a 2x7 rectangle of acacia planks in the center of the front of your main structure, then build 3-block-tall walls with white terracotta, leaving a space for a door in the center.

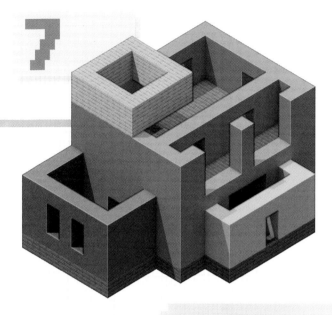

A block to the right of your entrance hall, add a 5x5 square of acacia blocks. Use purpur blocks with purpur pillars around the edges to build a tower 10 blocks tall. Add an edge of upside-down purpur stairs on top and fill in the roof with purpur blocks. Carve out two windows on the front of your tower and add glass panes. Create window ledges with quartz blocks, slabs and stairs, and add End rods on both sides.

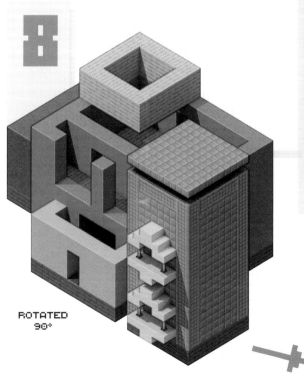

ROTATED 90°

FRONT

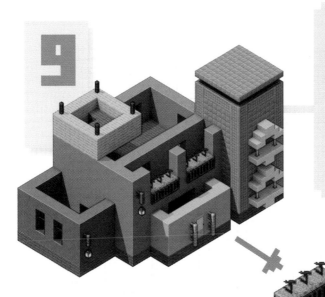

9

Build planters on your upper balcony with grass blocks boxed in by acacia trapdoors. Plant some flowers in them. Then add a variety of fences to the front of your casita, with lanterns dangling from a couple of them, and add 4 crimson fences to the corners of your cherry planks square. Add doors to your build.

Go to the back of your casita and add acacia trapdoors to the sides of the windows, with upside-down acacia stairs below each one. Add an acacia fence in the center with a lantern. On the green side of your build, use warped stairs and fences to build window frames. Add glass panes to all of your windows.

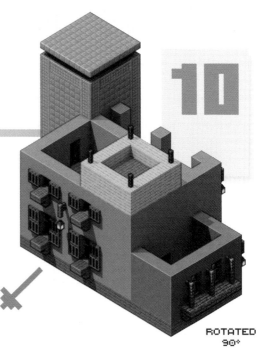

10

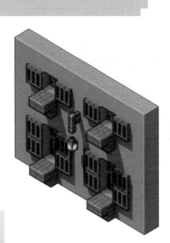

ROTATED 90°

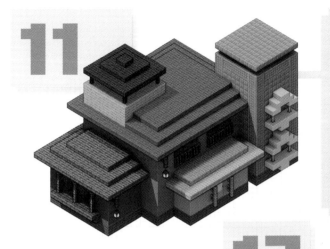

11

Each roof is built in the same way. Start with slabs overhanging the walls. Go up a half-block level at a time, 1 block in, up to three times. Fill in the rest of the flat section on top. Use crimson slabs on the cherry room, acacia slabs on the yellow section, warped slabs on the green area and birch slabs on the entrance.

12

Give your casita even more color by adding a range of azalea leaves, pink glazed terracotta, cherry leaves and vines growing up the edges of your building.

13

Go to the back of your build and add a 3x5 outdoor patio with bricks. Above it, add 2 stone walls to the corners, then 2 crimson fences. Build a balcony on top with crimson blocks and slabs, and add crimson fence gates around the edge with a lantern.

PANDA SANCTUARY

Who isn't a little obsessed with pandas? With different personalities –
including playful, lazy and worried – they're fascinating, for sure. If you
want to observe them more closely, then why not build them a sanctuary?
Just make sure to fill it with plenty of bamboo – pandas love to eat!

1

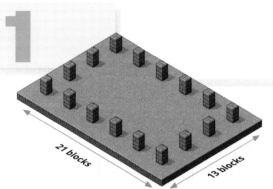

Start by building a rectangle of 2-block-tall pillars with stone bricks. Each pillar should have 3-block spaces between them, and there should be four pillars on the short sides and six on the long sides.

21 blocks

13 blocks

2

On the outside edges of each pillar, add another stone brick block with a stone brick stair on top. Note that the corners have two outside edges.

3

Fill in the spaces between all of the pillars with two rows of white wool, leaving a space empty in the center of the front wall. That will be the entrance.

4

Either side of the entrance, add 4 jungle planks on top of the pillars, then add 2 planks to each of the other pillars.

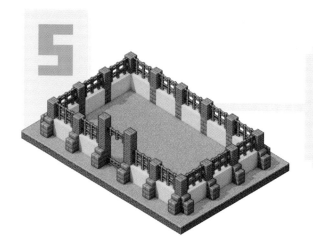

5

At the entrance, build a row of jungle fences 1 block down from the top, and add jungle fence gates at the bottom. Then add two rows of jungle fences between all of the other pillars.

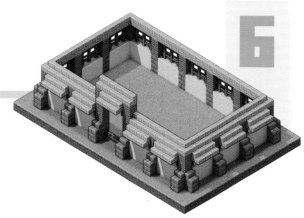

6

Add a ring of bamboo mosaic stairs around the top of your walls and above the entrance. Then add 3 stairs beside each other, outside every top layer of fences, including the ones above the entrance.

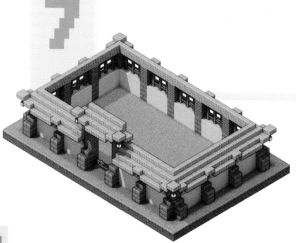

7

To finish the outside of your sanctuary, add 1 bamboo mosaic slab in each space where there's a jungle plank pillar. Then place 3 slabs staggered above each corner as well as the sides of the entrance, with a lantern dangling beneath the center slabs.

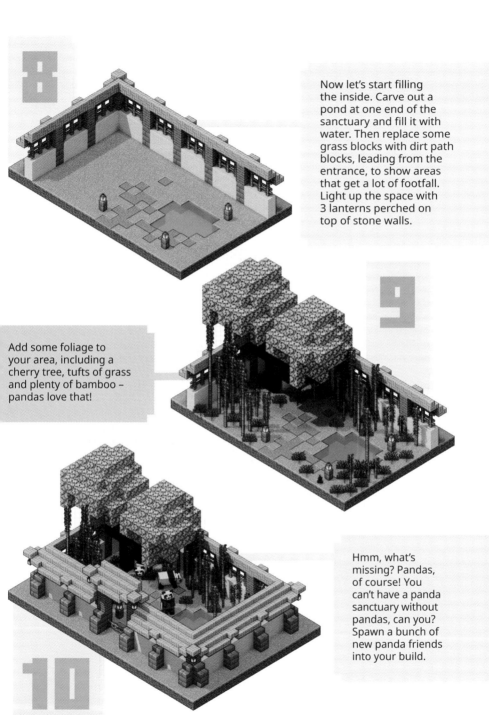

Now let's start filling the inside. Carve out a pond at one end of the sanctuary and fill it with water. Then replace some grass blocks with dirt path blocks, leading from the entrance, to show areas that get a lot of footfall. Light up the space with 3 lanterns perched on top of stone walls.

Add some foliage to your area, including a cherry tree, tufts of grass and plenty of bamboo – pandas love that!

Hmm, what's missing? Pandas, of course! You can't have a panda sanctuary without pandas, can you? Spawn a bunch of new panda friends into your build.

VERTICAL FOREST

Want to bring an urban tower block to your Overworld but still want it to blend in with its surroundings? Then this build is for you! With plenty of room inside, all your friends will be begging for their own floor within this block of apartments. Just imagine the view from the top!

DIFFICULTY:
★★★★★
🕐 1 hr

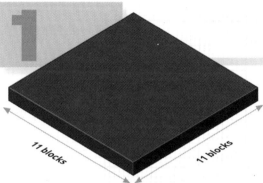

Begin by building a 11x11 square of gray concrete blocks for the floor of your base.

11 blocks

11 blocks

Next, build a 3-block-tall pillar on each corner of your build. Add another pillar in the center of three sides and a doorway arch in the middle of the front wall.

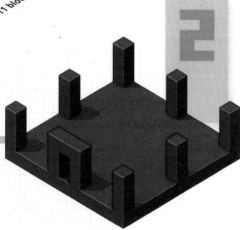

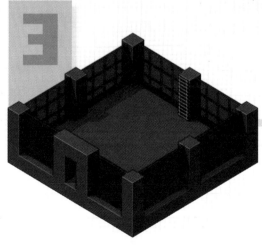

Fill in the spaces between the pillars with black stained glass panes. Add a ladder up the back central pillar so you can get up to the next floor.

33

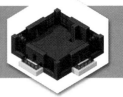

Build a 13x13 floor with gray concrete directly on top of your last floor. Leave a hole above the ladder on the ground floor so you can access this new floor.

Using gray concrete, build a pillar on each corner and one for the ladder, 3 blocks tall. In the center of each edge, build a 5-block-wide wall with space for a doorway in the middle. Outside of each doorway, build a ledge with white concrete blocks, 2 blocks deep and the same width as the walls.

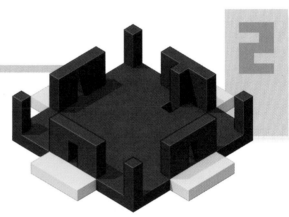

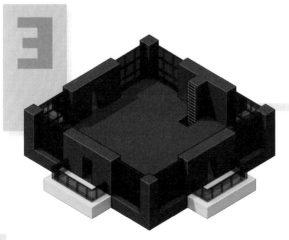

Fill in the spaces between the pillars and walls with black stained glass panes and add more as barriers around each balcony, 1 block high. Add a ladder to the back pillar to get upstairs.

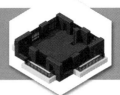

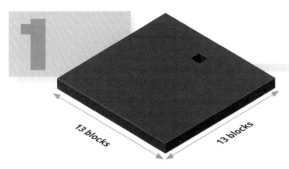

1 Build another 13x13 floor directly on top of your last one, with gray concrete. Leave a hole so you can continue your ladder from the floor below.

2 On the same side of each wall, build a 4x3 gray concrete wall with a doorway 3 blocks in from the corners. Then in the center of the spaces left, build 2x3 walls. Add a pillar at the back for the ladder. Outside the building, add 8x2 white concrete ledges, 1 block in from the corner where the doorways are.

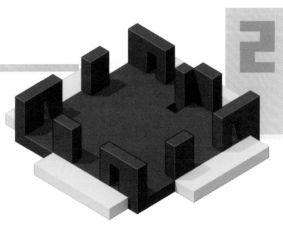

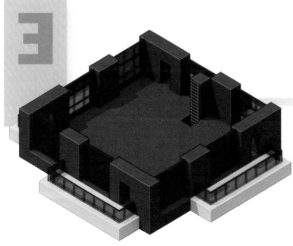

3 Use black stained glass panes to fill in the rest of the walls and add a barrier around the balconies, 1 block high. Add a ladder to the back pillar.

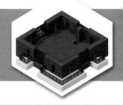

1

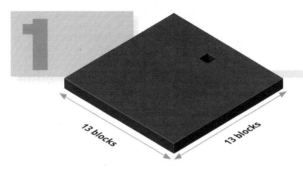

13 blocks

13 blocks

You know the drill by now! Build yet another 13x13 floor on top of your last one, leaving a hole for where your ladder is on the floor below.

This time, build walls with gray concrete, extending out 5 blocks from each corner, with a doorway facing out of each side. Add a pillar at the back for the ladder. On two opposite corners, build a white concrete balcony that extends around the corner, then at the other doorways, add 3x2 ledges.

2

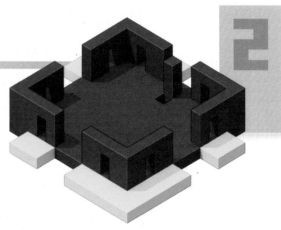

3

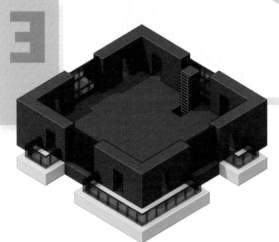

Add black stained glass panes to the gaps in the walls and 1 block high around the edges of the balconies. Then add a ladder to the back pillar to get upstairs.

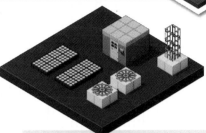

1

Repeat sections 2–4 twice more until you have an entire tower block. Add a flat roof on top with gray concrete, then build a 3x3 room, 2 blocks tall with light gray concrete. Give it an iron door and a stone button, and top it with smooth stone slabs. Add a couple of 2x2 iron block air vents, topped with rails in a circle to complete the look. Place a pair of 2x4 rectangles of daylight sensors, then finish off with a 2x2 iron block square topped with iron bars.

2

Now for the forest element! Grab every green leaf block from your inventory and place them in between the balconies and sometimes cascading from them, up every side of your build, until it looks as if your build is half-tree. You can even add some azalea leaves for a hint of pink!

RUBBER DUCK PARTY BOAT

Ever dreamed of throwing a celebration on your very own rubber duck party boat? No? Well, you will now! Gather your friends for a quacking afternoon aboard this ducky express, or pull up a chair and relax beside the water – that is until a drowned crashes your party!

DIFFICULTY:

⏱ 15 mins

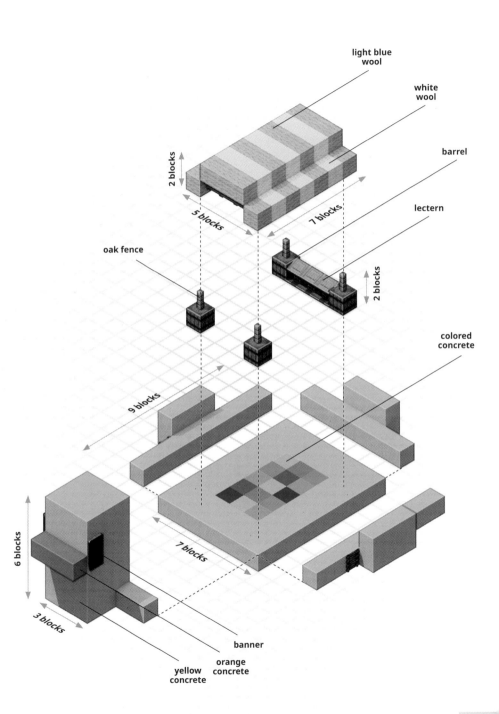

light blue wool

white wool

barrel

lectern

oak fence

2 blocks

5 blocks

7 blocks

2 blocks

colored concrete

9 blocks

6 blocks

7 blocks

3 blocks

banner

orange concrete

yellow concrete

STEAM TRAIN

CHOO-CHOO! All aboard the Overworld Express! Grab some coal and stoke the fires to bring this steam engine to life. Sure, it won't actually take you anywhere, but just look at how majestic it is. You could even add some carriages onto the back and turn it into an engine-ious base!

DIFFICULTY:
★★★★☆
🕐 35 mins

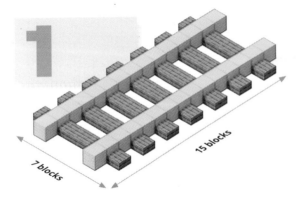

First let's build the train tracks for your engine to sit on. Use iron blocks for two rails, 15 blocks long, with 3 blocks between them. Then use oak slabs to create the sleepers, 1 block apart.

15 blocks

7 blocks

Above the iron rails, add a polished blackstone block between each of the sleepers, and then add a stone button to the outside of each of them. Fill in the space between these blocks with spruce planks.

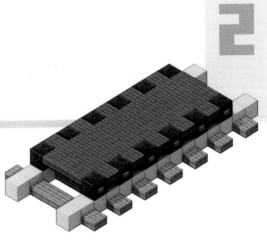

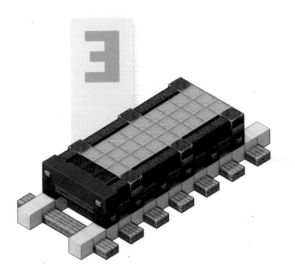

Add a line of red concrete at the front of your train with a stone button on both sides. Then add 3 blocks of polished blackstone directly behind it. Along each side of your train, add 3 blast furnaces, facing inward, and add anvils to the spaces between them. Fill the middle of the train with waxed oxidized copper.

At the front of the train, add a polished blackstone block in the middle, with upside-down polished blackstone stairs on each side and 3 more blocks behind them. Build a 3x4 rectangle of waxed oxidized copper in the middle, then place more around the back of your train, leaving a space at the end.

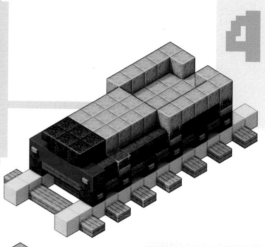

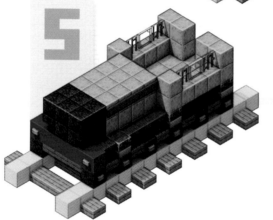

Build another layer of polished blackstone and waxed oxidized copper on the front of the train. Add spruce signs along the copper sides. At the back, place a glass pane between 2 iron bars on each side, and then fill in the rest of the walls with waxed oxidized copper.

Place polished blackstone blocks and stairs at the front, followed by waxed oxidized copper blocks with waxed oxidized cut copper stairs on both sides. Extend the walls at the back of your train up 1 block and fill in the gap above the doorway. Then add 3 waxed oxidized copper blocks at the front and back of that section.

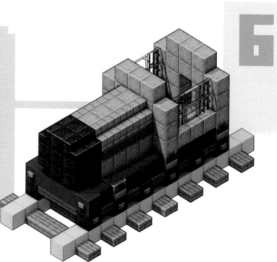

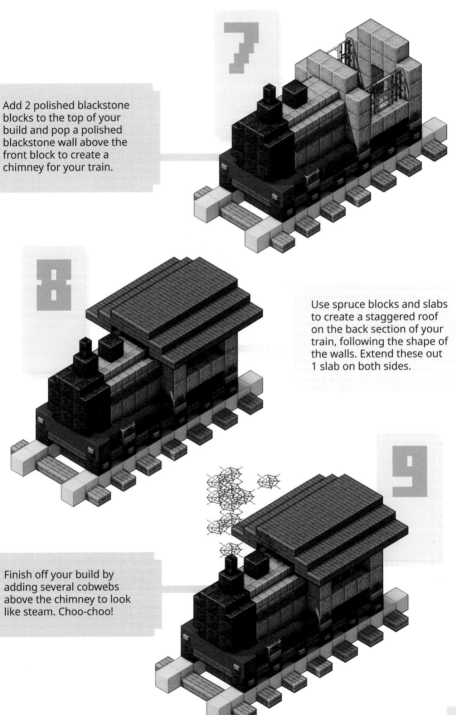

7

Add 2 polished blackstone blocks to the top of your build and pop a polished blackstone wall above the front block to create a chimney for your train.

8

Use spruce blocks and slabs to create a staggered roof on the back section of your train, following the shape of the walls. Extend these out 1 slab on both sides.

9

Finish off your build by adding several cobwebs above the chimney to look like steam. Choo-choo!

RIB-CAGE HIDEOUT

This build is really the bare bones of a build! Get it? If you love everything spooky, then this rib-cage base is the one for you. Of course, it will do little to keep any hostile mobs out, but surely just the look of it will be enough to scare them off. No? Fine. At least it looks cool!

DIFFICULTY:
★★★☆☆
🕐 25 mins

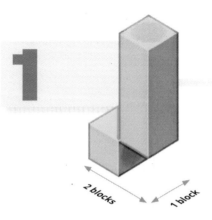

1

What do you make a rib-cage base out of? Bone, of course! Place 1 bone block, then to the side of it, leave a block free at the bottom, then stack 3 bone blocks.

2 blocks 1 block

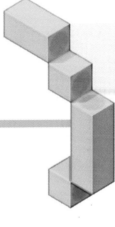

2

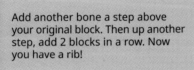

Add another bone a step above your original block. Then up another step, add 2 blocks in a row. Now you have a rib!

3

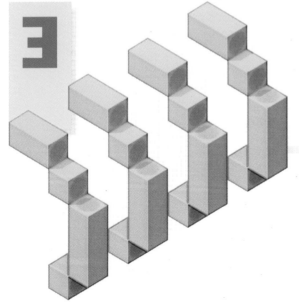

Repeat the first two steps three times, leaving 2 blocks of space between each rib, until you have four of them.

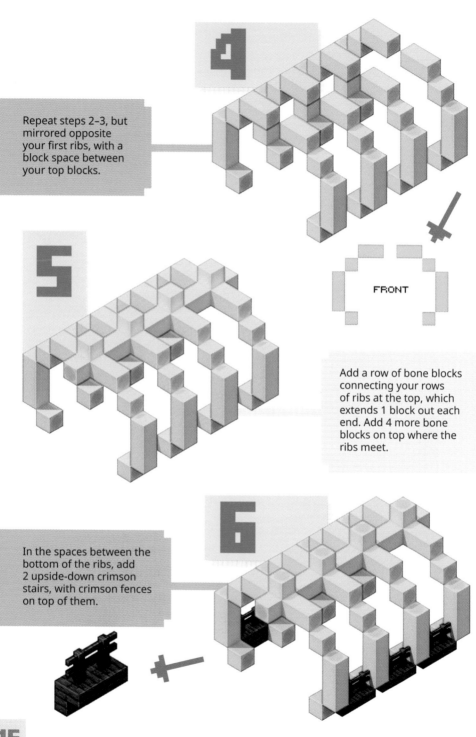

4 Repeat steps 2–3, but mirrored opposite your first ribs, with a block space between your top blocks.

FRONT

5 Add a row of bone blocks connecting your rows of ribs at the top, which extends 1 block out each end. Add 4 more bone blocks on top where the ribs meet.

6 In the spaces between the bottom of the ribs, add 2 upside-down crimson stairs, with crimson fences on top of them.

7

Add a menacing touch to your base by adding some iron bars around your entrance. Then stack up some barrels for storage.

8

ROTATED 180°

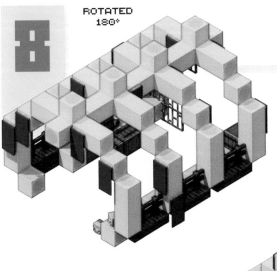

Decorate your ribs with red banners at random intervals to make it look a bit meatier (gross, right?). Then add some piglin heads to the back entrance to ward off intruders.

9

Light up your build with lanterns dangling from chains and a soul campfire to give your base an eerie glow.

RAPUNZEL'S TOWER

Thankfully, you won't need a trapped girl with ridiculously long hair to climb this tower. Seriously, someone give that girl a head massage! This tower is the ideal hideout from hostile mobs. Just close your door and there's no way anyone will reach you up there! Plus it's cute!

DIFFICULTY:
★★★★☆
🕐 45 mins

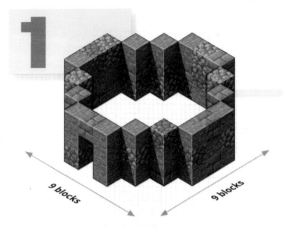

1

9 blocks

9 blocks

Use a mixture of stone, stone bricks, mossy cobblestone, mossy stone bricks and cobblestone to build the bottom of your tower 3 blocks tall in a rough circle.

2

With the same mixture of blocks, build the next level of your tower, 3 blocks tall and 1 block in from your last layer.

3

Build the main section of your tower 1 block in from your last level and 9 blocks tall. Gradually phase out your mossy blocks and cobblestone until you're using mostly stone blocks, with a few stone bricks toward the top.

Build a platform of birch planks the same size and shape as the middle section of the tower. Then add upside-down stairs around the outside edge, making it the same size as the base layer. Add another 2 upside-down stairs below each side of your straight edges.

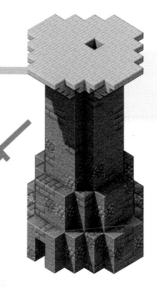

FRONT

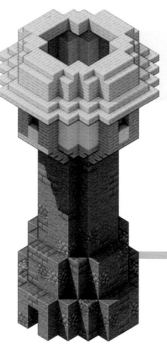

On each straight edge of your upper tower, build an arch of birch planks 4 blocks tall and 3 across. In the center, add a white wool block to the bottom and fill in the rest with light blue stained glass panes. Then build the diagonal walls with white wool.

Start building your roof by adding a ring of cherry stairs around the top layer of your walls. Build a layer of cherry planks on top of the cherry stairs. Then place cherry stairs on top and add a ring of cherry planks inside of them.

7

Continue your roof, adding a layer of cherry planks 1 block in from the last. Then, to the straight edges only, add a layer of cherry stairs. Behind these stairs, add two layers of cherry planks with a ring of cherry stairs on top.

8

9

Below the windows, add planters made with cherry trapdoors around grass blocks. Then decorate the rest of your tower with vines, cherry leaves and birch leaves.

Finish your roof with a square of cherry planks 1 block in from your last layer, with a square of stairs on top. Complete with 2 cherry planks stacked on top. Add a cherry door to your entrance, with a cherry block and 2 slabs above it, and then add birch fences either side.

CAMPERVAN

Build a base away from home with this adorable campervan! Find an incredible spot to park your van and get building. The interior of this campervan has everything you need to survive in the wilderness, whether you use this as a temporary shelter or your main base.

1

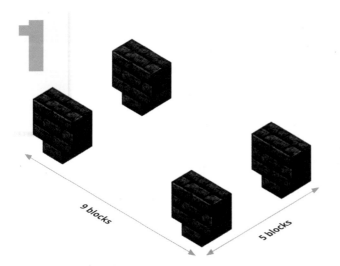

Use 2 polished blackstone brick stairs, upside down and back to back, plus 2 polished blackstone blocks on top to create the four wheels. Build the front wheels 3 blocks apart, then add two more 5 blocks behind.

9 blocks

5 blocks

Use smooth stone slabs, half a block up from the floor, to create a rectangle that connects your wheels and extends 2 slabs in front and behind them. Add two more layers of slabs, a block in from the edges of the first layer.

2

3

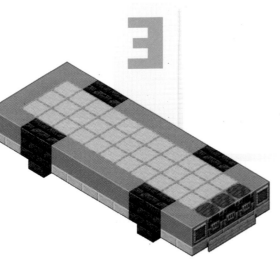

Add 3 blast furnaces to the front of your campervan, on top of the single slabs. Then use orange concrete to fill the rest of the spaces on that level. Place 2 item frames for headlights and 3 birch signs for a bumper.

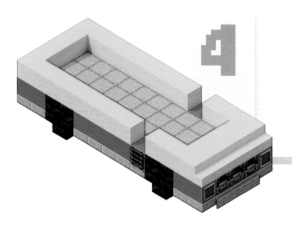

Place a row of quartz stairs at the front of the campervan with a row of smooth quartz blocks behind it. Add a layer of quartz blocks above the remaining orange blocks, leaving a block space behind each of the front wheels. Then pop a ladder below the gaps.

Place iron doors in the gaps, then add 1 smooth quartz block in front and 2 behind them. Add 5 more smooth quartz blocks to the back as shown. Fill in the rest of the spaces with glass panes, placing the front panes 1 block away from the front. Pop a lever beside both doors.

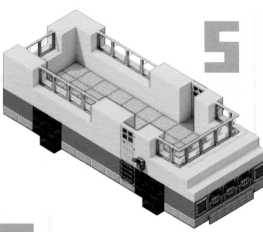

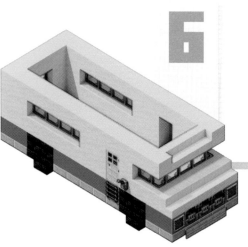

Add a layer of smooth quartz blocks directly above the previous layer, except for at the front, where you switch 3 blocks out for quartz stairs.

Along the front of your campervan, add a row of quartz stairs, then three rows of smooth quartz blocks. Behind this, add a row of smooth quartz slabs, then extend this layer backward, filling the space between the walls until you reach the back.

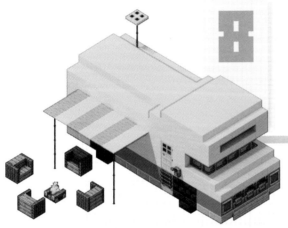

Build a striped awning sticking out from above your windows with white and light blue carpets. Prop it up with iron bars. Then add a satellite dish to the top of your campervan by placing an iron trapdoor on top of 2 iron bars. Build chairs around a campfire using oak stairs and spruce trapdoors.

INTERIORS

Fill the inside of your campervan with as many items as you can. You can add a kitchenette with a cauldron, a furnace and a crafting table, and a little dining area with a spruce trapdoor and 2 oak stairs. For the bedroom, you can place trapdoors for side tables and even pop a large chest above the bed for extra storage. How many things can you fit in your campervan? Don't forget to add a stone button on the inside of each door and add 2 quartz stairs at the front for the driving seats.

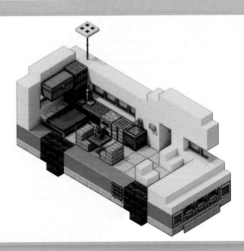

CAMEL STABLE

Gosh, it's hot in the desert, and without a frozen dessert in sight to cool you down! How do camels survive in it? Give yourself and your trusty camel a place to chill out in this desert base, complete with a stable. There's even space to home an entire camel family!

DIFFICULTY:
★★★☆☆
🕒 35 mins

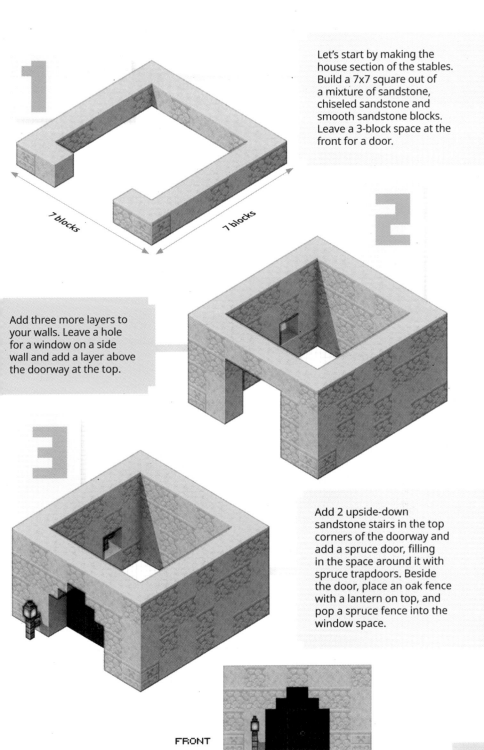

1

Let's start by making the house section of the stables. Build a 7x7 square out of a mixture of sandstone, chiseled sandstone and smooth sandstone blocks. Leave a 3-block space at the front for a door.

7 blocks

7 blocks

2

Add three more layers to your walls. Leave a hole for a window on a side wall and add a layer above the doorway at the top.

3

Add 2 upside-down sandstone stairs in the top corners of the doorway and add a spruce door, filling in the space around it with spruce trapdoors. Beside the door, place an oak fence with a lantern on top, and pop a spruce fence into the window space.

FRONT

Place a line of oak buttons above the doorway. Use smooth sandstone to fill in the ceiling, leaving a hole for a ladder. Add a layer of smooth sandstone slabs around the front of the build, extending 1 block back on both sides.

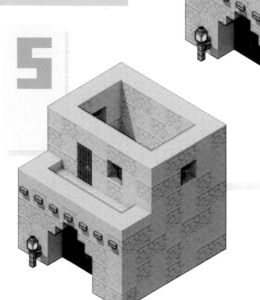

Build the upstairs of the house 3 blocks tall and 2 blocks shallower than your downstairs. Add three holes with oak fences in them for windows, and add a spruce door leading to the balcony.

Fill in the ceiling with smooth sandstone, then use smooth sandstone slabs to add an edge around the roof. At the front, add two layers of 5 slabs in the center, then add 3 slabs on top, using a mixture of different sandstone blocks. Add 3 oak buttons to the front.

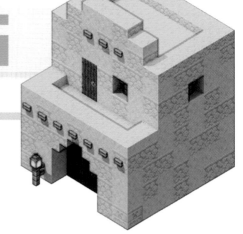

Now for the stables! Extending from the back of the house, build a wall 4 blocks tall and 10 blocks wide out of smooth sandstone and sandstone.

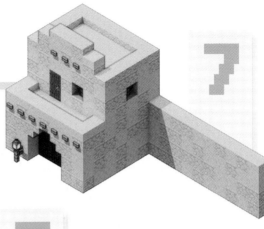

A block back from the front of the house, build four pillars, 4 blocks tall with 2 blocks of space between them. Then in between the top blocks of each, add 2 upside-down sandstone stairs facing each other, then place a slab on top of each of them. Connect the arches to the back wall by adding sandstone walls at the end.

Create a wooden roof with lines of campfires – be sure to put out the fires with a shovel! Add fence gates to each archway. On the central pillars, add fences with a lantern dangling from them. Finish by adding stacks of hay bales inside.

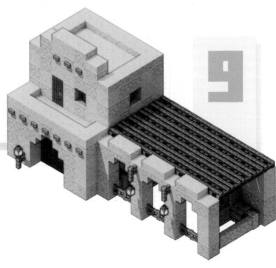

RAMEN SHOP

Give your Overworld its very first takeout restaurant with this cyberpunk ramen shop. Sure, all the ramen tastes suspiciously like stew, but who doesn't love stew? The kitchen is stocked with everything you need to cook, so you'll be whipping up tasty meals in a jiffy!

DIFFICULTY:
★★★☆☆
🕐 35 mins

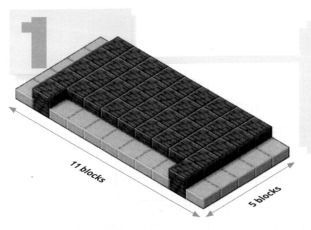

Build a 9x4 rectangle of polished deepslate, then add 1 more block to each end at the front. Add a line of smooth stone slabs between the 2 polished deepslate blocks and add a row on either side.

11 blocks

5 blocks

On the front row of polished deepslate blocks, add a line of alternating smokers and chiseled deepslate blocks with iron trapdoors on top. Behind this, leave a block, then add 4 smokers, 2 cauldrons and a crafting table to complete the kitchen area.

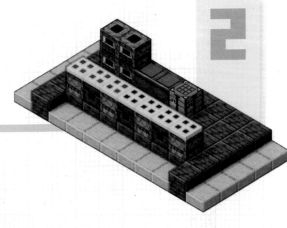

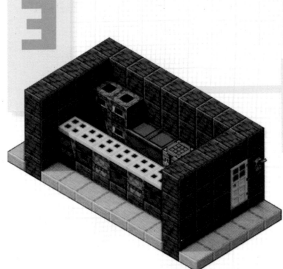

Build up the walls around your kitchen with polished deepslate, then add an iron door with a lever beside it so that you can get inside to cook!

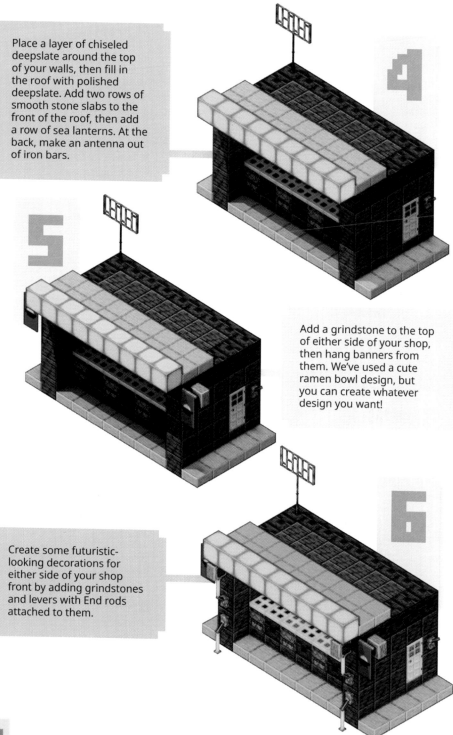

Place a layer of chiseled deepslate around the top of your walls, then fill in the roof with polished deepslate. Add two rows of smooth stone slabs to the front of the roof, then add a row of sea lanterns. At the back, make an antenna out of iron bars.

4

5

Add a grindstone to the top of either side of your shop, then hang banners from them. We've used a cute ramen bowl design, but you can create whatever design you want!

Create some futuristic-looking decorations for either side of your shop front by adding grindstones and levers with End rods attached to them.

6

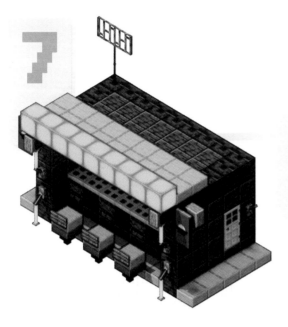

7

Give your customers the option to sit down and eat by adding 3 hoppers with smooth stone slabs on top, then place warped signs on the backs to make them look like chairs.

BANNER

To create the ramen banner, first pop the following items into your inventory: 1 red banner, 2 red dye, 1 white dye, 1 black dye and a bordure indented banner pattern. Then use a loom to add the patterns shown below one at a time, layering them up by putting the same banner back into the crafting section each time.

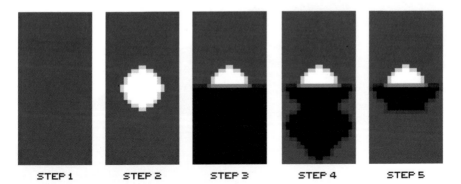

STEP 1   STEP 2   STEP 3   STEP 4   STEP 5

NETHER JAIL

If you thought the rib-cage base was a little cagey, wait until you see this build! Inspired by bastion remnants and complete with a dangling jail cell, this Nether jail is the perfect spot to throw any mob that dares to cross you in this dimension. Let them be warned!

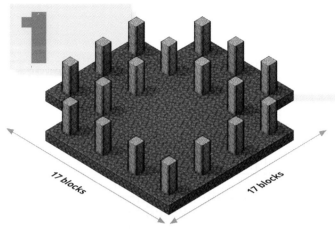

1

Build a square of 3-block-tall polished basalt pillars with four on each side and 3 blocks of space between each pillar. Add three more pillars to both of the far sides of the build, 3 blocks out from the pillars already there.

17 blocks

17 blocks

2

Use a mixture of polished blackstone bricks, cracked polished blackstone bricks and gilded blackstone to fill in the spaces between the pillars around the outside of your jail. Leave a section empty at the front for your entrance. Connect the remaining internal pillars to the outside walls.

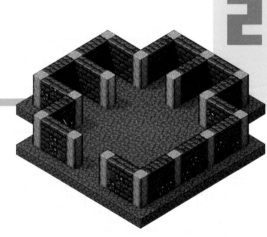

3

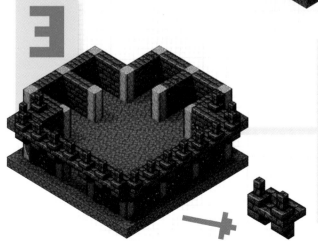

Above the front of your build, add two rows of polished blackstone brick slabs that stick out a block from the sides. Every other block in the outside row, add another slab with a polished blackstone brick wall on top. Below each of those, add upside-down polished blackstone brick stairs.

Create your jail cells by adding 2 upside-down polished blackstone brick stairs, facing inward, at the top of each internal pillar, then connect them with a polished blackstone brick slab. Add iron bars to your cells to trap in your prisoners.

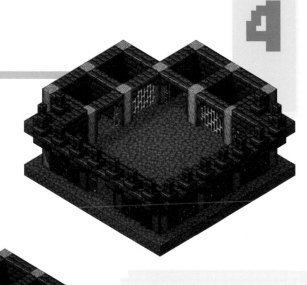

5

Of course, four cells aren't enough for your jail! Add a ceiling to each of your cells using the same mixture of blackstone blocks, then extend the walls and pillars up by 3 blocks.

Add upside-down polished blackstone brick stairs to the insides of your pillars, again with iron bars beneath them. Then add a mangrove slab ledge around the front of the upstairs cells, ending 2 blocks before you reach the outside walls of your jail. At these ends, add ladders so you can get upstairs.

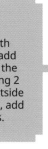

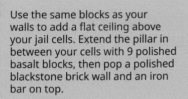

Use the same blocks as your walls to add a flat ceiling above your jail cells. Extend the pillar in between your cells with 9 polished basalt blocks, then pop a polished blackstone brick wall and an iron bar on top.

7

8

Around the outside of the roof, add upside-down polished blackstone brick stairs on every other block. Above them, build a layer of polished blackstone brick slabs. Then on the slab above each of the stairs, add another slab and top with a polished blackstone brick wall.

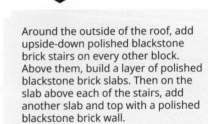

FRONT

Extending out from the top of your tall pillar, use polished blackstone bricks to add 3 blocks with a slab at the end, then add 1 upside-down stair beneath it. Underneath the third block, add a chain, then build your 3x3 cage with mangrove slabs and two layers of iron bars. Finish by adding soul lanterns around the jail.

9

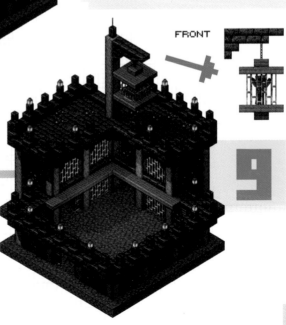

RAINBOW BASE

Who doesn't love seeing a bright rainbow in the sky? Well, with this base, you can see a rainbow every day in Minecraft. Just be sure to hide your chest of gold somewhere less obvious than on either end of your base — particularly if you decide to build it in the Nether!

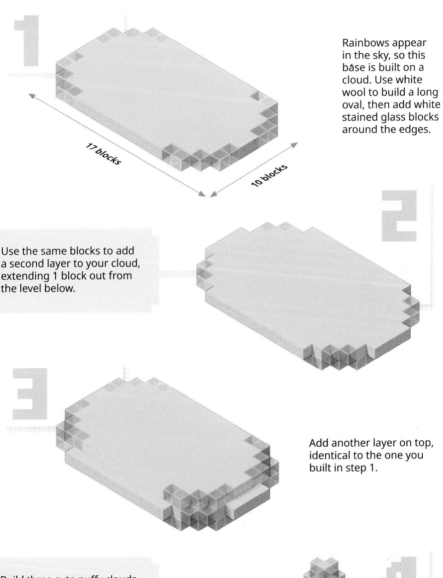

Rainbows appear in the sky, so this base is built on a cloud. Use white wool to build a long oval, then add white stained glass blocks around the edges.

17 blocks

10 blocks

Use the same blocks to add a second layer to your cloud, extending 1 block out from the level below.

Add another layer on top, identical to the one you built in step 1.

Build three cute puffy clouds around your main one. Create a plus sign with white wool and add another block to the center of each side. Surround each point of the cloud with white stained glass blocks to make more plus signs around the sides.

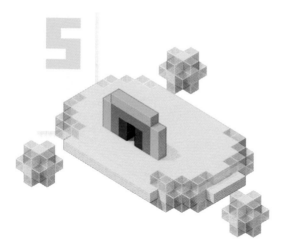

Begin to build your rainbow shape, starting with two pillars of red concrete, 2 blocks tall with a space between them. Then build an orange concrete arch over the top of these, followed by a yellow concrete arch with the corners missing.

Continue to build up your rainbow with arches of colored concrete, going from lime to light blue to purple.

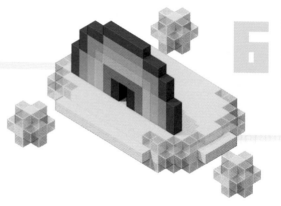

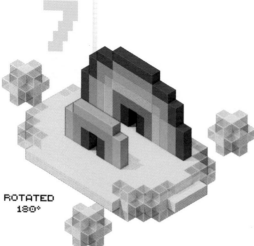

ROTATED 180°

Go to the back of your cloud and begin building your second rainbow 5 blocks behind the first, but with the colors in reverse. Start with purple concrete pillars, followed by light blue, then lime concrete.

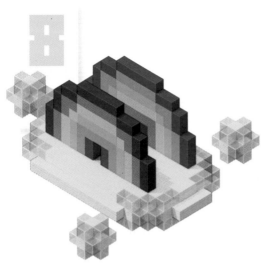

Finish your second rainbow by adding yellow, orange, then red concrete arches until your two rainbows are the same size and shape.

Now for the rainbow roof! Use stained glass blocks and follow the shape of the walls to build one layer at a time, starting with orange, then yellow, lime and finishing with blue.

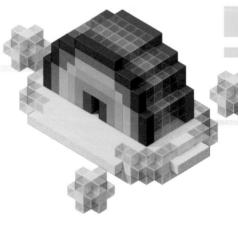

Finally, add a crimson door to your base on both sides, then place 2 crimson fences with End rods on top to light up the outside of this epic base.

BUMPER CARS

Bring the mayhem of bumper cars to your game with this fun build. Use ice for the floor and boats for the cars, and you've got yourself a wild ride to go on with your friends. To make it *really* chaotic, arm yourselves with swords and compete to destroy each other's boats first!

DIFFICULTY:

★★☆☆☆

🕐 20 mins

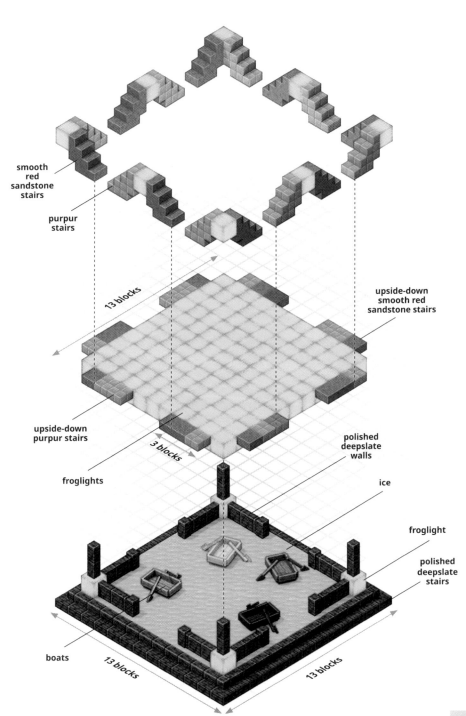

smooth red sandstone stairs

purpur stairs

13 blocks

upside-down smooth red sandstone stairs

upside-down purpur stairs

polished deepslate walls

3 blocks

froglights

ice

froglight

polished deepslate stairs

boats

13 blocks

13 blocks

FLOWER POT HOUSE

If you love flowers, this build will make you wet your plants with excitement!
With a base inside the flower pot and unbe-leaf-ably large flowers on top,
this house will look gorgeous in whatever biome you decide to put your
roots down. So what are you waiting for? Get growing!

DIFFICULTY:
★★★★☆
🕐 1 hr

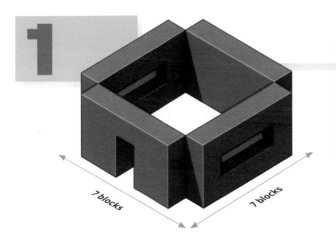

1

Begin by building the terracotta flower pot. Build a 7x7 square without the corners. Make each wall 3 blocks tall and leave spaces for a door and wide windows on two walls.

7 blocks

7 blocks

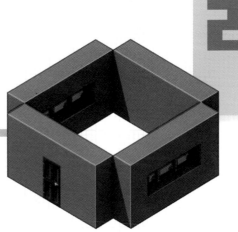

2

Add a dark oak door and glass panes to the spaces.

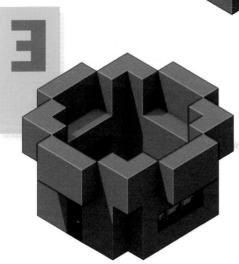

3

Add 3 more terracotta blocks to the center of each side, 1 block out from the walls, then fill in the corners in line with the walls below. Build another layer on top.

4

Add a ledge around the edge of your flower pot, 1 block up and 1 block out from the level below. Fill in the middle with grass blocks to create a roof. Leave a hole at the back for a way up from inside.

5

Add decorative planters around the base of your plant pot using grass blocks surrounded by spruce trapdoors and upside-down spruce stairs. Choose a selection of flowers for them.

6

Now it's time to start building the flowers. Using lime concrete, build an arched stem coming out of the right side of the pot.

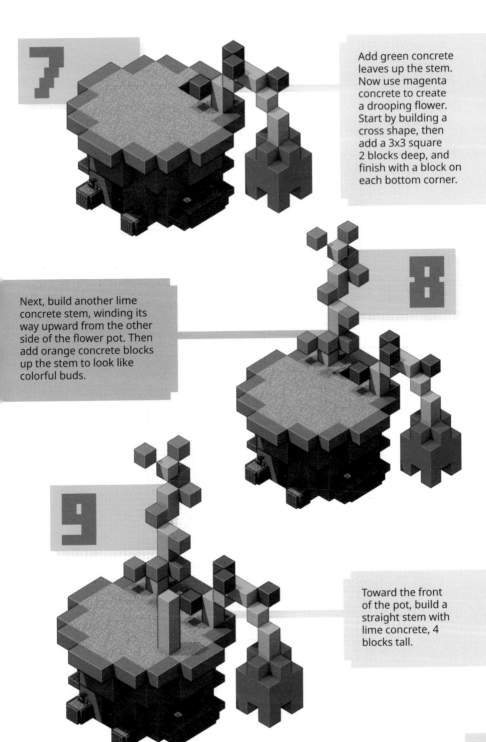

7

Add green concrete leaves up the stem. Now use magenta concrete to create a drooping flower. Start by building a cross shape, then add a 3x3 square 2 blocks deep, and finish with a block on each bottom corner.

8

Next, build another lime concrete stem, winding its way upward from the other side of the flower pot. Then add orange concrete blocks up the stem to look like colorful buds.

9

Toward the front of the pot, build a straight stem with lime concrete, 4 blocks tall.

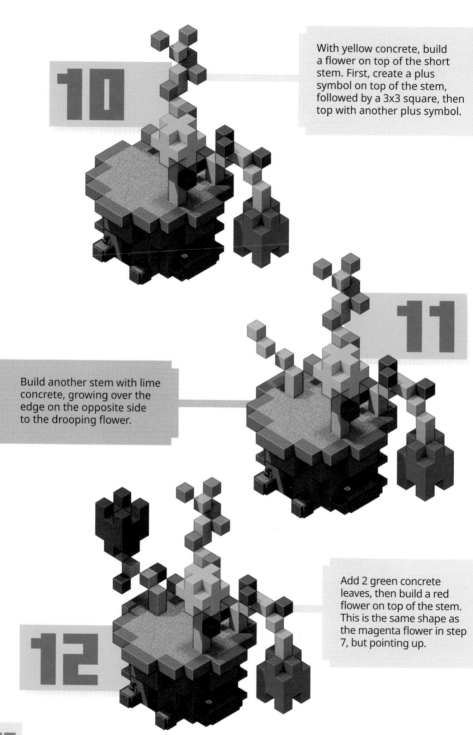

10

With yellow concrete, build a flower on top of the short stem. First, create a plus symbol on top of the stem, followed by a 3x3 square, then top with another plus symbol.

11

Build another stem with lime concrete, growing over the edge on the opposite side to the drooping flower.

12

Add 2 green concrete leaves, then build a red flower on top of the stem. This is the same shape as the magenta flower in step 7, but pointing up.

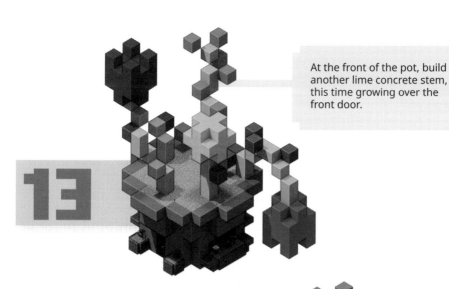

At the front of the pot, build another lime concrete stem, this time growing over the front door.

13

14

On top of the stem, use light blue concrete to build a 3x3 square. Above this, add a ledge 1 block out around the edges, without the corners. Another layer up, add a block above the corners and sticking out from the center of each side.

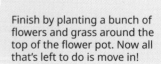

Finish by planting a bunch of flowers and grass around the top of the flower pot. Now all that's left to do is move in!

15

THREE LITTLE PIGS

When a wolf comes to pay a visit, which house do you think is the safest to hide in? Luckily for these three little piggies, this wolf can't get into any of them and they don't attack pigs in-game. Phew! In fact, the biggest threat to these pigs' safety is ... YOU! But you wouldn't eat them, would you?

DIFFICULTY:
★★★☆☆
⏱ 45 mins

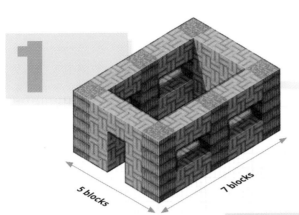

First, let's build the house made of straw. Well, kind of! Use hay bales to create six pillars, 3 blocks tall, then fill in the spaces with bamboo mosaic blocks, leaving gaps for four windows and a door.

5 blocks

7 blocks

Add a bamboo door and glass panes to your spaces, then stack up more bamboo mosaic blocks in a triangle on each end of your build.

Beginning 1 block below the tops of your walls, build your roof with a mixture of bamboo and bamboo mosaic slabs. Stagger the slabs up until you reach the top, and then add bamboo stairs on either end, facing inward.

Now it's time to build a sturdier house (though you'd be pretty safe in any of them). Build six pillars of oak logs and fill in the gaps with oak planks, leaving space for a door and four windows.

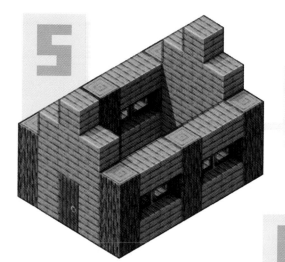

5

Add a spruce door and glass panes to your windows. Then build a triangle of oak planks on top of the walls on the front and back of your build.

6

Use a mixture of spruce and oak slabs to build your roof, starting 1 block below the side walls and staggering upward. Add spruce stairs to the top, at the front and back, facing inward.

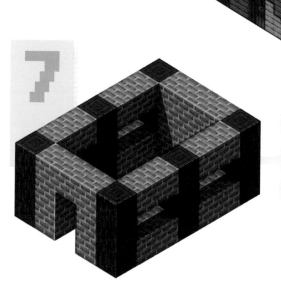

7

Finally, let's build the sturdiest of piggy homes! Use dark oak logs to build six pillars, then fill in the gaps with bricks, leaving space for a door and four windows.

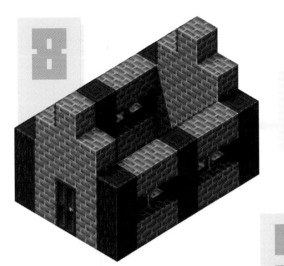

8

Add a dark oak door and glass panes to the spaces, then add a triangle of bricks on top of the walls at the front and back.

9

Use a mixture of stone brick slabs and brick slabs to create the roof, starting 1 block below the top of the walls and staggering upward to meet in the middle. Up top, add stone brick stairs on both ends, facing inward.

10

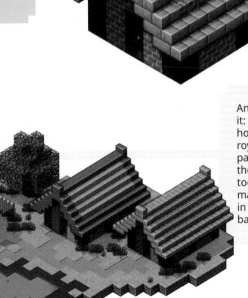

And there you have it: three adorable homes fit for piggy royalty! Add a dirt path connecting the three buildings together and maybe even throw in a mud pit for bathtime!

NARROWBOAT

Ahh, doesn't it sound dreamy, living on a river, watching the sun set and waving smugly at the zombies on the riverside? KNOCK, KNOCK. Wait, what? Where did that drowned come from?! URGH, is there nowhere safe in the Overworld? At least this base looks pretty. Just don't answer the door!

DIFFICULTY:
★★★★☆
🕐 35 mins

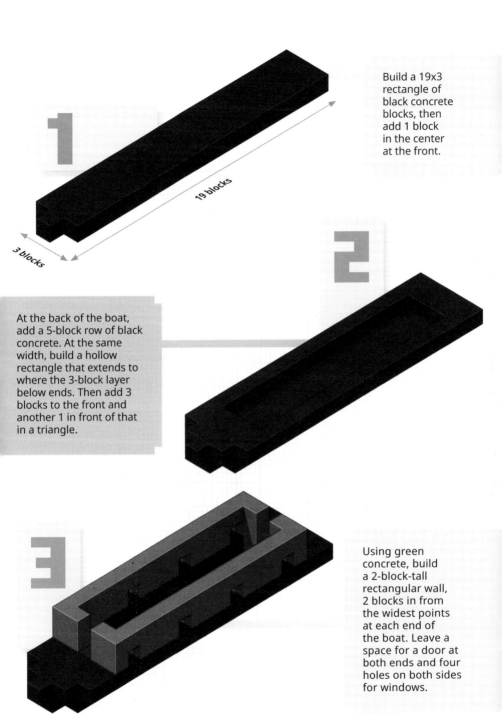

1 Build a 19x3 rectangle of black concrete blocks, then add 1 block in the center at the front.

19 blocks

3 blocks

2 At the back of the boat, add a 5-block row of black concrete. At the same width, build a hollow rectangle that extends to where the 3-block layer below ends. Then add 3 blocks to the front and another 1 in front of that in a triangle.

3 Using green concrete, build a 2-block-tall rectangular wall, 2 blocks in from the widest points at each end of the boat. Leave a space for a door at both ends and four holes on both sides for windows.

Add a mangrove slab above each hole, with a mangrove fence gate below them in the open position to look like shutters. Add oak buttons to both sides of the fence gates.

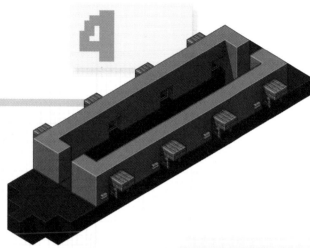

At the very front of the boat, add a mangrove plank and slab. Follow the outline of the boat, placing 6 upside-down mangrove stairs, facing backward. Add an oak door, as well as oak fences on the mangrove stairs beside the wall.

Move to the back of the boat. Add 2 upside-down mangrove stairs on each side, facing the boat. Then out of the back, add 2 more, facing inward with a block space between.

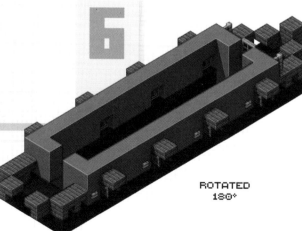

ROTATED
180°

Add a blast furnace to the space at the back of the boat, then build a rudder from it using iron bars in an S-shape. Add one more iron bar above the rudder to use as a handle. As you did with the front, add an oak door and 2 oak fences.

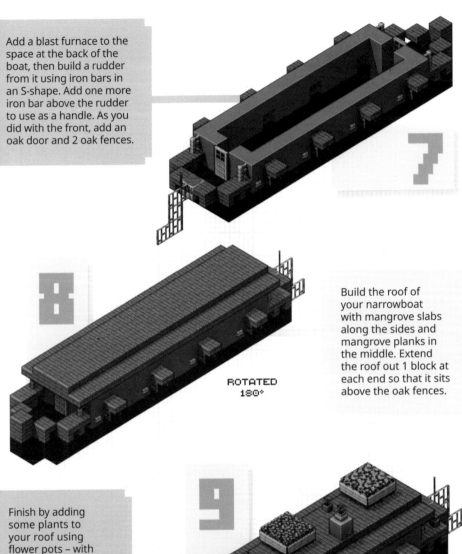

7

8

ROTATED
180°

Build the roof of your narrowboat with mangrove slabs along the sides and mangrove planks in the middle. Extend the roof out 1 block at each end so that it sits above the oak fences.

9

Finish by adding some plants to your roof using flower pots – with some placed inside decorated pots – and leaves surrounded by oak signs.

UFO

Oh, no! Evil aliens have come to steal all the cows of the Overworld! Oh wait, it's just a statue? That's totally out of this world! No one would ever dare mess with you near this UFO for fear that aliens would abduct them. It's the perfect defense. Plus it comes with a cow for milk!

DIFFICULTY:
★★★★☆
🕐 40 mins

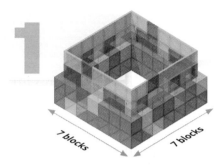

1

7 blocks 7 blocks

Use mostly green stained glass blocks with a few lime ones thrown in to build a 7x7 square, 2 blocks tall. Use the same color stained glass panes to add another two layers on top, gradually adding in more lime panes.

Build the next two layers, a block in from the first with mostly lime stained glass blocks and a couple of yellow thrown in. Then add another two layers of stained glass panes, adding in more yellow as you go up.

2

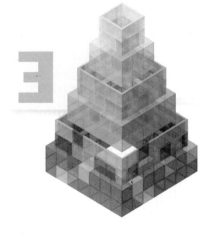

3

A block in from the last layer, add another two layers of yellow stained glass blocks, with a couple of white stained glass blocks on the top layer. Build two layers of stained glass panes on top, adding more white until it's fully white on top.

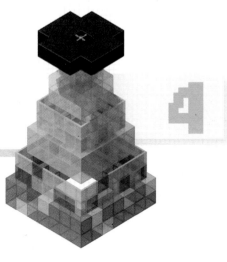

4

Build a 5x5 square without corners on top of your glass pyramid, using gray concrete. Remove the middle block and add an oak fence inside.

Up 1 block, add a circle of gray concrete around the outside of the layer beneath, 2 blocks wide. Then add a ring of froglights on top along the outside edges.

Add another circle of gray concrete above your froglights, the same size as the concrete level below. Then a block up, add a rim around the opening with 3-block lines on each side.

Around the outside of the froglights, add a ring of lime stained glass blocks with smooth stone slabs placed on the tops and bottoms.

Add lime stained glass blocks on top of the raised lip, then place a 3x3 square of them a block up to fill the hole.

Decorate the top and bottom of your UFO with stone buttons placed around the edges of the gray concrete.

Now to beam your cow up! Spawn a cow in the center of your glass pyramid and attach a lead to it. While holding the lead, click on the fence above to tie it there, which will hoist your cow up toward your UFO!

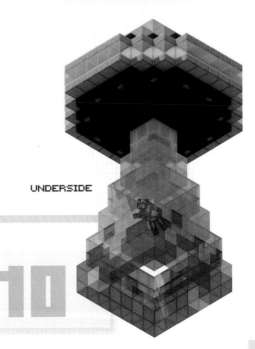

UNDERSIDE

COMBINATION CHALLENGES

Congratulations! You've completed all the builds in this book. You must be quite the builder — but you're not done yet! Let's see if you're up to a new challenge: combining builds together to create new ones.

Listed below are a series of combination challenges. For each of these challenges, we want you to combine the builds using the guides and tips included in this book. How you combine the builds is completely up to you: You can resize the builds, pick new blocks or improve the design as you see fit.

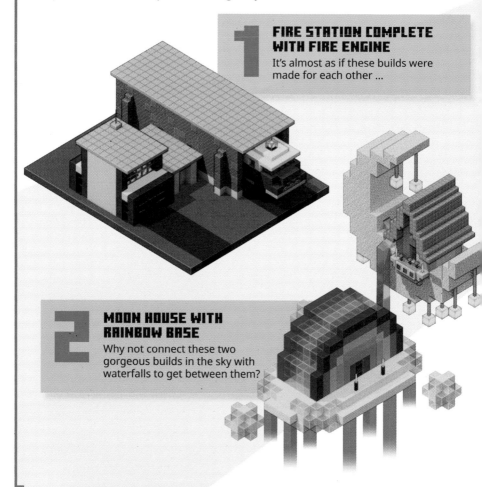

1 FIRE STATION COMPLETE WITH FIRE ENGINE

It's almost as if these builds were made for each other ...

2 MOON HOUSE WITH RAINBOW BASE

Why not connect these two gorgeous builds in the sky with waterfalls to get between them?

RUBBER DUCK NARROWBOAT

If you're quackers about ducks and want to keep drowned from crashing your parties, then why not combine these two builds?

VERTICAL FOREST WITH RAMEN SHOP

How better to feed everyone living in your vertical forest than with a built-in ramen shop?

NETHER JAIL WITH RIB-CAGE ROOF

Want to make your Nether jail even creepier? Add some giant bones above it!

GOODBYE

Well done! We've just created some incredible builds together. Which one was your favorite? Was it the duck party boat? Or perhaps the cow-snatching UFO?

Whichever one you enjoyed the most, remember the fun doesn't have to stop here. All of these builds are begging to be tinkered with and changed in whatever way your imagination tells you to.

Don't shy away from getting creative and straying from the instructions within these pages. That's the joy of Minecraft, after all! It's all about your creations and your journey.

It's OK to make mistakes and take chances – that's how you'll learn. Keep on creating exciting new builds and exploring thrilling new ideas!

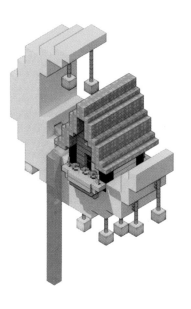